*Where the Deer Were*

# *Where the Deer Were*

### Poems by

## Kate Barnes

### *With woodcuts by Mary Azarian*

David R. Godine · Boston

*First published in 1994 by*
DAVID R. GODINE, PUBLISHER, INC.
Post Office Box 450
Jaffrey, New Hampshire 03452
*www.godine.com*

*Library of Congress Cataloging-in-Publication Data*
Barnes, Kate, 1932–
Where the deer were: poems / by Kate Barnes;
with woodcuts by Mary Azarian. — 1st ed.
p.   cm.
PS3552.A6812W54   1994      94-13801
811'.54—dc20      CIP

ISBN 0-87923-984-0 (hardcover)
ISBN 1-56792-117-5 (softcover)


FIRST SOFTCOVER PRINTING, 2000
*Printed in the United States of America*

*This book is dedicated with love to my godmother,*
*Hope Crouch Nash.*

# CONTENTS

*Excuses to Stones*

*Time Out*

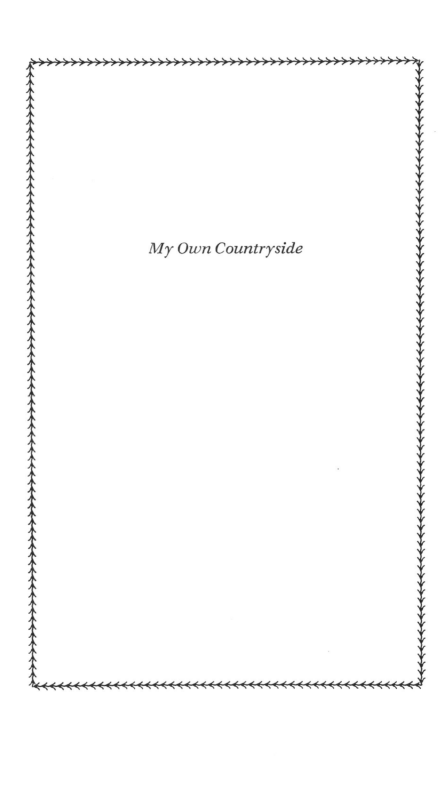

*My Own Countryside*

## Coming Back

Coming back to my own countryside, I find
the farm again. It is night. Under this wallpaper
of willow leaves and birds, I know there is
an old one with loops of small roses. The sound of leaves
outside in the darkness is not the weeping tongues
of that new willow, it is sighs from the ghost
of the box-elder that stood here before, the one
we children once scared ourselves into believing
that we could see moving, creeping almost invisibly
toward the bedroom window where we sat looking down
at fireflies.
      I can hear my dead father
still grieving and raging downstairs like the Minotaur
in the depths of the palace cellar; like water,
my mother's voice goes on soothingly.
           *Sleep now.*
The hoofs of a wooden horse trot through the house,
the red horse from a merry-go-round who once
rocked in the woodshed.
      *Sleep now.*
          I reach my hand
toward him, and feel the breath from his carved nostrils
warm on my palm.
      *Sleep now.*
        His upreared head,
with its long waving forelock and solemn glare
like the sculpted bust of a Victorian poet,
turns to me.
      In a moment he will speak.

## The House Asleep

By day my house says to me, "Clean me, clean me!"
The compost bucket growls, "Put on your boots,
get ready for the trek out through the snow."
The rugs cry for the vacuum cleaner, the floor
says, "Sweep me, and now please wash me, I want a pure soul."

But at night, once I have turned out all the lights,
I can't get to sleep, I have to wander around,
like a ghost, through the warm rooms of my sleeping house.
I put a stick of birch in on the ashes
and something begins to whisper in the stove,
but I can't quite hear the words.
                                        The travelling moon,
almost full, looks down from above the roof
to the white hills; she walks silently
over the cold fields. The house is filled
with her milky blue fire, two times reflected,
through which I wander in my white nightgown
brushing past the rose geranium leaves.
Suddenly the guitar hanging on the wall
speaks by itself. One string gives a loud twang,
and then it is all silence again, and light,
the smell of the leaves, the wordless dreams of the house.

6

## Night Light

Lying in bed in the pitch black, a little breathing
    underlies my own;
it is my dog on the floor; we are both alive here.
And I struggle with the old illusion; there is
    something else in the room,
a story in the darkness—if I wake up I can
    write it down.
It is the light of the purple grape, the deep glowing light
that emanates from my black horse's flank, the knee-
    length, straight,
shiny black hair of the round-faced girl in Sonora
dancing with her groom at the fiesta while all the
    aunts sat and smiled;
or it is the telephone pole with *Black Beauty* stamped
    on it, or the thin black dog
named Ink Spot, or the one sleek all-black cow with black
    horns—
in the herd of Holsteins always a silhouette; it is the
    screaming games
of murder in the dark house, the quick uncertain
    kiss in the pantry, the running feet;
they are all here in the darkness with me, they crowd
    me with their light.

## Children

It was all founded on a child's unspoken wishes,
formed early from an Edwardian frontispiece.
Lancelot carries Guinevere away from the fire
sitting sideways before him on his saddle bow.
She looks straight ahead; the wind blows her long hair back;
she is wearing her royal nightgown. Is it the flames
at the stake that make the sky lurid behind them or only
sunset? One thing is clear, they are never going
to get down from that horse.
                                    But they did get down
and bought themselves an old house on the side
of a mountain slope where the world was green and lonely
around them, and they lived in the cool rooms
like simple tribesmen who have overrun
a Roman villa; horses in the rose garden, ponies
led through the tiled hall, children's dirty faces
grinning down from the trellis among the grapes,
the shingles falling.
                            And the four wild children,
think of the secrets they had, and never told!
The springs they found, the pot plants that they grew
in a tiny, hidden canyon where the grown-ups
never came, the nights they crept from their beds
and climbed into the oak tree by the gate—
twice as high as the roof—to sleep on the rimless
platform of the treehouse they had built,
suspended between the sky and the distant ground
where the slightest movement of the branches rocked them
and they heard the cries of owls in the grove below
sounding like ghosts in the darkness.

Their mother knew
nothing about it. It was spring. She had gone
to dinner with her husband at the nearest house,
a half mile up the slope. They came home on horseback.
The horses danced in broken moonlight, and she thought,
"We are like Virgil's souls in their world of shadows.
Could we have died already and not know it?
Do we only think we are riding through these oak trees,
silently over the leaf-mold?"
                              And the dreaming children,
asleep among the branches over their heads,
rang like the strings on the guitars suspended
silent on the wall when someone plays
in the same room, and the drowsing instruments
answer the parent air with a sleepy chiming.
The tall tree rocked them, the light wind hushed their sleep.
All night long they heard the stirring leaves
whispering like fathers and mothers in the dark.

## Future Plans

When I am an old, old woman I may very well be
living all alone like many another before me
and I rather look forward to the day when I shall have
a tumbledown house on a hill top and behave
just as I wish to. No more need to be proud—
at the tag end of life one is at last allowed
to be answerable to no one. Then I shall wear
a shapeless felt hat clapped on over my white hair,
sneakers with holes for the toes, and a ragged dress.
My house shall be always in a deep-drifted mess,
my overgrown garden a jungle. I shall keep a crew
of cats and dogs, with perhaps a goat or two
for my agate-eyed familiars. And what delight
I shall take in the vagaries of day and night,
in the wind in the branches, in the rain on the roof!
I shall toss like an old leaf, weather-mad, without reproof.
I'll wake when I please, and when I please I shall doze;
whatever I think, I shall say; and I suppose
that with such a habit of speech I'll be let well alone
to mumble plain truth like an old dog with a bare bone.

## The Brown Sweater

Knitting a sweater for your unrequiting love,
you knit hair into it twice so that whichever
way he turns it, some will lie by his heart.
Black hair, fine and small, Irish hair,
hair that has its instructions, that has been programmed
to get itself wound tightly around his affections
and lead them to you like horses brought up from pasture.

I touch the sweater made of undyed wool
from brown sheep in Iceland. The soft stuff feels
as resilient as moss. I look at you busily wishing.
Your face is not screwed up with concentration;
it only deepens with the same sudden deepening
produced by the sight of a train passing under a bridge
or a falling star, each good in your mind for one wish.

In the evening you read French cookbooks looking for
    something
to delight him. In the morning you tell me your dreams
about him. Every night you dream about him!
Every day- all day—you are listening for his truck.
And this has gone on for a year! How can I say:
God's will be done, or: that man alone is happy
who makes the best of what the Fates send him?
                                        I can't.

In the face of your longing, in the face of your
    suffering need,
consolation of any kind would be
an injury. You hug the sweater and stare
across the top at me with the look of the doe
I once saw plunge in the lake leaving a pack
of stray dogs yelping behind her in our hayfield.
It was still summer, though late, the water not
too cold, the dogs not too determined. She swam
bravely away, growing smaller and smaller, until
she reached the opposite shore and disappeared,
safe in the thicket.
                    Give me magic, give me hope!
Give me the powers of bone-deep wishes, the lucky
omens, the white horse, the first star of night,
the doe ten miles by land from her howling griefs,
the blue-black hair, springing from a head of dreams,
twining into a strand of brown yarn and bringing
love and luck to the wearer—without his knowledge.

## Long Distance

The long distance
telephone wire
pulses gently

with its weight of
overflowing news, and we
tell each other

what we've been doing
lately, what old friends
we've seen, what is in bloom

in our gardens; the rose here,
*Reine Victoria,*
with its round, heavy

buff-colored blossoms
hanging perfumed
from the bending stalks,

and the red lilies
that hold up their cups
to the sky, and the mass

of tiger lilies
whose lowest buds
are turning orange

in the rainy mist
outside on the lawn
that hides the edge

of the woods, and the stone
walls of the field, and the face
of the barn so that all

these incarnations
swim in a kind
of detective story

and we can't tell exactly
what our words mean, or even
what we are trying

to say: Did you think
it was true, then? What else
could I have done?

## Women Alone

Smelling of horses and soap, you climb into bed
beside me. What you are looking for is company
and a chance to tell me about your so-far unfortunate
heart's progress with a disregarding man

who lives across the lake. We are like two children
who fall asleep telling stories in the dark
or like the team of chestnut workhorses sharing
their one big stall in the barn. In the morning you

will go on loving and wishing, and I will go on
listening to you—and what is the use of that
when the one thing wanted, the one thing necessary
is Adam and Eve standing bemused and enchanted

in the green light under the strange, jewelled tree?
A recumbent stag watches them from the fresh grass;
the leaves shade them; their bodies are pale as wool;
they look at one another, and she hands him a bitten apple.

# Four Victorian Coatsworths Speak from Their Graves

## I

### William Coatsworth

Of the four children in our family,
two killed themselves.
It was my fate to manage the grain elevator,
to earn and then divide the money,
to live on in this bustling American city
when I was really only happy in the far west or Europe,
a born lover of nature and the arts.
I wish I could have written or painted
but I hadn't the strength for everything.

When my ulcers became so painful
that I had to stay in a dark room for two months—
and they were still no better—
I prepared carefully,
I told my wife and each child how much I loved them,
I shot myself with a small gun so that my body would be less
    frightening.
My hold on life had been worn through
but I was always generous and brave.

## II

### Ida Reid Coatsworth

When my husband killed himself,
I thought I would never be happy again
but two years later James Isham,
my high school sweetheart, a widower now,
asked me to marry him.
Of course, I talked it over with my grown daughters
and, when they both said they thought I had better not,
I told James I was sorry,
and lived on for forty years
like a gentle ghost in my gray silk dresses,
loved and forgotten,
a pensioner in my children's houses.
Oh, passerby,
walking on the grass beside my grave,
take hold of your life with both hands.

# III

## Jenny Coatsworth

I suppose it was wrong of me
to drink that poison—
it wasn't an easy way to die—
but, really, what else could I do?
There was no place for me in this world
or, if there were one, I never could find it.
I was shy, and dark, and tall,
not a fashionable type for the period.
(I should have been little and blond like my sister, Mally,
plump, with natural curls,
able to talk and laugh with anyone.)
I loved books and the arts.
I did go to Radcliffe College for a year
but I couldn't settle down, I felt too strange there.
I studied sculpture in Paris with Barye
who said I had a nice talent
but that no young lady could expect to work in stone;
and I sang with Madame Marchesi
who said Miss Coatsworth's voice was unusually true,
but not big enough to fill a concert hall.
I came back to Buffalo and had a suitor I adored;
he was a young professor, the leader of our Browning circle.
At last I had someone I loved and could talk to.
I tasted happiness, I found out what it was like;
but then my sister Mally married him
although I begged her not to take him away
when she had so many beaux
and I had only him.

I hope Mr. Emerson is right
and that our souls return.
Perhaps, in another time,
there would be more chance for someone like me.

18

# IV

### Mrs. Caleb Coatsworth

When I was seventeen
my parents married me to the oldest son
of an old Philadelphia family who were rich
and proud, living in their fine brick houses;
and he was a dashing young man,
a sport with a diamond stickpin,
who drove matched bay trotting mares,
the fastest pair of horses in the city.
When he tried to kiss me,
I didn't know what to do
and, after the wedding,
when we got into that big bed,
I was so scared that I giggled and giggled wildly,
unable to stop myself,
until he held a pillow over my face
and went about his business.
I couldn't breathe, I thought I was being murdered.
When he died, five years later,
I tried to grieve but, really, I couldn't.

Then I married Caleb Coatsworth
and I suppose he was a sportsman, too.
He was always in trouble with his family
for his polo ponies and tandem carts;
his older brother had to pay his debts.
But there never was a kinder man than Cale.
Everyone loved him.
I know they laughed at me all those years
because of the way I followed him about
like someone's pet lamb.
     I am glad
to know we are still together in this grave.

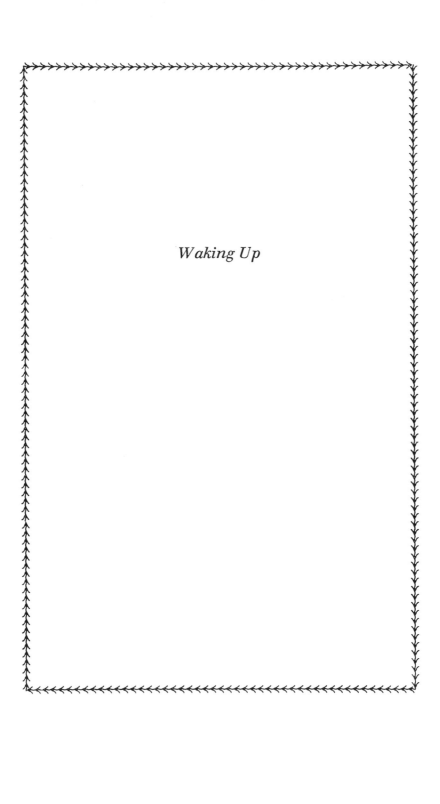

*Waking Up*

## Imagining It

At eighteen, in Paris,
I woke up out of a dream
just before dawn, and stepped through the long window
from my cold room with its red silk walls.
Shivering a little in my dressing gown,
I leaned on the balustrade
and, look, overnight a light snow had fallen;
no car had driven over it yet, it lay in the street
as white, as innocent, as snow on the open fields.
Then something approached with a calm rhythm
of hoof-beats made softer by the snow, the sound
of a quiet heart. It was a heaped-up wood cart
pulled by a gray horse who walked along slowly,
head down, while the driver
sat at the back of one shaft and hunched over
to light his cigarette.
                        From above, I saw clearly
the lit match in the old man's cupped hands, its glow
on his long jaw, the small well of flame
between his living palms like the flare
of the soul in the body. He went on
down the street, and the sky went on
growing lighter, and I saw how he left
his dark tracks behind him on the whiteness
of the snow, just the lines of the two wheels,
slightly wavering, and the dints of the horse's hooves
between them, a writing in an undiscovered
language, something whose meaning
we feel sure we know, and still can't quite
translate.
              When I stepped inside again,
I stopped thinking about love for a minute—I thought about it
almost all the time then—and thought instead
about being alive for a while in a world
with cobblestones, new snow, and the unconscious
poem printed by hooves on the maiden street.

Of course I was not yet ready to be grateful.

## At Home

My mother, that feast of light, has always sat down,
composed herself, and written poetry, hardly
reworking any, just the way she used to
tell us that Chinese painters painted; first they
sat for days on the hillside watching the rabbits,
then they went home, they set out ink and paper,
meditated; and only then picked up their brushes
to catch the lift of a rabbit in mid-hop.

"If it didn't come out I would throw it away."
                                        Oh, she
is still a bird that fills a bush with singing.
The way that she touches her tea cup, the look she gives you
as you sit across from her, it is all a kind
of essential music.
                    I also remember my father
alone at the dining-room table, the ink bottle safe
in a bowl, his orange-red fountain pen in his big
hand. The hand moved slowly back and forth
and the floor below was white with sheets of paper
each carrying a rejected phrase or two
as he struggled all morning to finish just one sentence—
like a smith hammering thick and glowing iron,
like Jacob wrestling with the astonishing angel.

# The Springs under the Lake

Oak trees stretched their branches from the stone pile
with the cows in their shade. Below, the ground was wet
as my mother and I pushed through a fringe of bushes
into water almost as warm as blood on that hot
July afternoon. Here and there, our feet
found jets of coolness where springs under the lake floor
streamed freshly upward.
                              My mother set out
in her stately breast-stroke, her head up like a turtle's.
I splashed at angles to her course, half dogpaddling,
half at a crawl. When I grew tired, I put
one hand on her shoulder.
                              At the mouth of the cove,
we paused, treading water, to pick water lilies
that floated on long stalks over the rafts
of their round leaves. We carried them, sopping and perfumy,
up toward the house where they would live a long time
in a wide bowl on the table, unfolding their cool
white petals every day and closing them
in darkness.
                              When we were halfway up the hill,
my mother stopped to look at a monarch butterfly
on a hawkweed that went on swaying softly
while the wings above it slowly opened and closed.
I watched her leaning over it so intently
in her rusty old black bathing suit; and then,
quite suddenly, quite without warning, the world
became alive, it seemed to breathe—the red-top
bending in the afternoon wind, clouds blowing north,
the water lilies lying tangled and dripping
in our arms, catspaws by the island, cloud shadows
on the hills, the thin orange and black wings
slightly trembling above the orange flower
that was moving too.

In a little while I couldn't
stand it any more. "What are you doing?" I asked,
and then I guessed it, something she didn't usually
mention, "are you thinking of things for a poem?"
She paused another moment before she said yes
quietly, as if she had just woken up
and needed to sleep longer.
                              The rest of the way,
I didn't talk. I could almost hear the words
combining in her mind, the lines gathering
by themselves like butter when it suddenly
starts to come, when it clumps up thick in the churn.

## The Knife's Edge

When I woke up this morning
I found I was writing a poem in my dream
and the only line I could hold on to
was: take nothing for granted.

So I will write down that one line
and go looking for the rest;
I will take nothing for granted.

When I walk out of the house the air is still
but I can see the wind getting up.
Now it is in the bushes on the skyline,
and now in the stand of poplars by the spring—
I hear it speaking in the shivering leaves—
and now, a minute later,
I feel it, blowing coldly in my face.

North-west wind,
must you blow down all these bright leaves—
red maple leaves above the hillside,
stippled poplar leaves glittering in front of them,
green-gold beech leaves, yellow birch leaves, subtle ash,
sumac like small flames in the pale grass?

And the wind says, "Yes,
I must get to work now,
I must blow them all down;
I must take nothing for granted."

I walk up into the wood
looking at the flickering light in the dry ferns.
The tree tops toss in the wind,
the branches bend, and the air is full of noises.
As I lean against the trunk of a big birch,
I feel the tree swaying right into the ground,
and when I tip back my head
to look straight up at the rushing clouds,
I am dizzy, I think I am falling into the sky—
and I think I hear my mother's voice
in the creaking of the branches.

My mother is ninety years old.
She sits all day in her brown armchair
in the corner of the warm parlor.
"I am wise now," she tells me,
"but it is a knife's edge."

# Epona

Waking up this morning, I found myself
still in a dream of washing a white mare
in the washing machine. She emerged
dripping, untroubled, her satin flanks
streaming, her surprising eyes—
the blue of Peking glass—
calm. She looked at me
for a moment, and then she galloped away.

                                      Later,
when I finished a poem or, no, it finished itself
on my paper, I went outside
among tangles of blue vetch, purple clover,
day lilies, spurges, and blooming milkweed
that smelled of honey. The field edges
were illuminated with their flowers, the farther hills
arched across the horizon
in waves of blue haze, and a narrow lake
lay bright and deep in the hollow of the land,
shining upward.
                     Someone seemed
to be tearing curtains in my rib cage, someone
seemed to be crying. On the poplar branches,
all the light leaves turned over
as a gust of the afternoon wind galloped away.

## The Phooka

A story begins to travel
in the night. It is never
seen by daylight. If you meet it
you can protect yourself
by putting your coat on
inside out. You might think
it was just a loose horse clattering
at the edge of the road or a dog
nosing the shed door. It isn't
safe to speak to it although
it doesn't do any harm
to bless yourself. "God bless us!" you say
and something disappears at the corner
near the wood. Where it was
you are aware only of a slight
stir among the branches—
                       and, above you,
the clouds reaching out from the hilltop
in long bridges you can see well
by the light of so many stars.

# The Old Ones

It's not hard to find them,
the old ones. They are there
in the farm graveyard, Ripleys, Snows,
and Harts. *Capt. Abraham Ripley, mariner,*
died in eighteen-six, *Hannah, his wife,*
eight years later. Their dark, narrow slate
has a poem at the bottom that starts
*Silent and low my habitation* . . . and then
disappears in the long grass.
                                    Behind them,
under pine branches at the back,
you see the earliest graves, unmarked
field stones, half covered with green moss.
There is an obelisk in the middle of the plot,
shoulder-high, with a stone urn at the top,
both yellow with lichen; and near that
a small, thick piece of white marble,
the gravestone of a Victorian infant,
carved in a relief so deep that it's almost
freestanding, a hand holding a bouquet
of roses and lilies-of-the-valley
that droop like willow branches
at the rim.
                        The graveyard is edged
with square granite posts which have lost the chains
that sagged between them. The surrounding tangle
contains old roses—dark pink rugosas—tiger lilies,
and day lilies. All around it,
the sloping blueberry fields stretch out for miles.
Among them, a clump of lilacs the size
of a cottage marks a cellar hole
where a dug well is still covered by a slab of stone
with a hole in it, that is itself
covered by a smaller stone.

There are shards
of flowered plates in the soil of our lawn, and even
some thin lustreware. In the spring thaw,
when the barnyard runs like a brook, I once picked up
a corroded metal circle, a green sun—
a big penny from eighteen-nineteen that a man
paid a full day's labor to get, and then lost,
and never did find.
                  At the top of the outcropped ridge
where two high fields meet, someone made his oxen
drag up a great rectangular block of granite,
like a natural altar, and set it into the wall
on the height of land so that he could sit there
at evening and look down on his whole farm,
the fields, the pastures, the house and barn,
the valley with its glint of river,
the translucent blue of the hills in the long light—
and I still walk up there at the end
of the afternoon as if I were climbing a stone stair
whose steps have been worn into hollows
by other feet.
            In the late fall—
when the blueberry harvest is long in, the hayfields cut
a second time, the kitchen garden bare, the flowers
dying in their beds— the souls stream up
from the darkening, uncovered ground and enter
the night wind. They are lonely then, they whistle
like starlings under the eaves, they rattle latches
in the dry wood of doors, they ask us
what we are doing with their fields, their lives, with our
land, our lives, what we are *doing*.

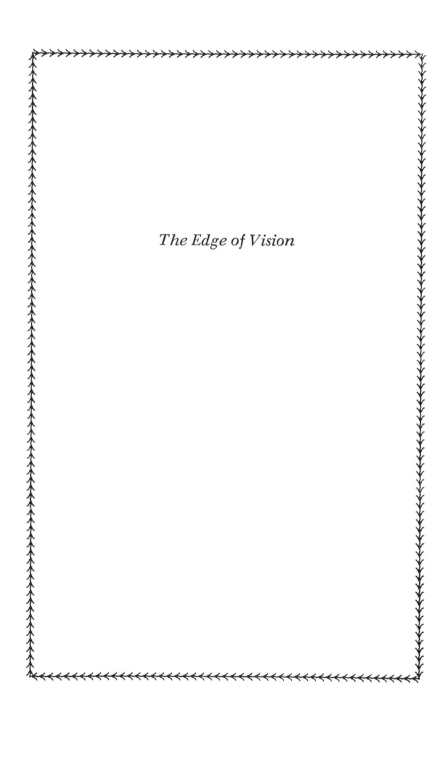

*The Edge of Vision*

## Inside the Stone

Up in the woods,
in the circle among the beech trees,
last winter one of the lumber horses split a stone
horizontally, with a clip of his big steel shoe.
It had seemed to be a plain gray stone,
but when it was opened a black wall appeared,
rusty at the edges, flecked with pale checks
like unknown constellations, and over all
floated wisps of blue-gray, trailing feathers of clouds.

I brush away the fallen leaves
and stare into the distance inside the stone.
If one could become a bird—
if one could fly into that night—
if one could see the circling of those stars—

and then the woods become very still,
the beech leaves blur at the edge of my vision.
I find I am bending lower and lower.

## Looking at Coins

## 1

We have to look at the Greek coins over and over,
turning them about in the light until at last
we begin to see something new in the sun's
edgeless circle, in the white face
of the moon
                    showing us rivers
like man-faced bulls, and bulls bellowing
as a big tunny swims up below them.
                              On the plain,
Victory drives her four-horsed chariot, while under her
in the world of dreams, Scylla, the dangerous mermaid,
grieving and raging still, points her trident; a chariot wheel
lies broken; a lion springs,
open-mouthed; the battle trophies stand heaped.

## 2

The ancient coins are like poems
that we don't yet understand.
We must have patience, we must wait
for their answers.
                    In that world of contained
intention, the bright swan
floats on the arching waves; the cuttlefish
curls up its tentacles like the tendrils
of a flower; the little hare
leaps over a cicada, which then springs up
onto a head of barley.
                              Pegasus beats his strong wings
through silver air; the girl in the sycamore
couples with the eagle; the griffin
clacks its beak and stretches
its long claws; the panther's face
stares from the incuse square.

Now the boy on the dolphin
parts the metal ocean carrying
his various blessings, while old Silenus,
squatting among the ivy, lifts the cup
once more to his thick mouth.

### 3

"Water is gold,"
says the shepherd on Naxos. "Water is best
of all things," said Pindar, "and gold
the dearest possession"—but this gold and silver
are almost immortal, far too old and alive
for us to possess them. Sometimes we see them
on a young gray horse's quarters, or pouring
in glitter on ripples, or they are shimmering
on the side of a dying trout, or gently shifting
in sunspots among the leaves when a summer wind
stirs the thick branches.
They have been traveling
more than twenty centuries to get here, turning
around and around again under the earth like dogs
who can never quite settle, like round
poplar leaves drifting down in circles
of silence and darkness. Now they have risen
into the light once more, and their images
flicker with fire, their words
are called "legends," their stories
tell themselves in our bones.

### 4

When we turn them over,
there is a stillness, an attention. It is the holy
faces that look out at us, the divine ones
look outward or turn to look
into the invisible distance, the world
disappearing into the edge of the coin, where Poseidon

gazes landward, Zeus to the thundercloud, Athena
tranquilly into the spear line.
Young Koré
stares sideways. She wears her harvest wreath
of twisted barley nodding with poppies, the having
and the forgetting. Her eyes are wide open. She looks
into two worlds at once. Her earrings
swing back along her neck, she is still
stepping forward. Her unseen foot

stays in the air, poised lightly.

## Delphiniums

Last night the breath of rain, and today
white clouds in a sunlit sky, a July
afternoon. Everything seems hushed
in the heat. The hummingbirds keep coming
on flying visits to all the delphinium flowers,
poking their long beaks into the dark spot
in the center of each blue blossom.
                                    Summer
wears away. In the field the hay is down,
and I see the old green tractor going round
and slowly round again, pulling the tedder
with its glittering toss of grass behind it. A small boy
in a straw hat drives it, sitting up straight, while his father
cuts the field above.
                    It is sleepy here
on the shadowy back porch. The two tractors
buzz and crawl on the long shimmering slope
behind the barn; nearby, a few pink poppies
nod among white daisies and buff-colored lilies
at my knees. The leaves
of the tall pear tree flash like small mirrors
in the slight stir of the air; two hummingbirds
thrum in the blue flowers by my ear.
                                    The day procedes,
however imperceptibly. In a little while,
light is edging the delphinium
through their pale blue petals, while darkness spills
from the center of each mass and from the sepals
of each blossom. They are like clouds that sail
near the sun, ringed with brightness, or souls
that surrender themselves to time. They drift
in the slow tide of the summer afternoon, a tide
so still that the world holds back for it: the hot bird
opens its beak, and doesn't sing; the cut grass hangs
in the air a moment, not falling; in the sea, the swimmers
must leave the warm surface of the water and dive
deep into the darkness and cold below them
before they begin to feel the current at all.

## The Night Tide

When we finally got to the beach house, the night tide turned.
The moon was setting beyond the marshes, Arcturus
still bright above the hill, no wind, and the salt river
moving back to the sea with a silent power
so deep that a yellow planet stood reflected
burning the same from the sky and its calm surface.
"Stay!" said the house, and the curtains touched our shoulders,
the broom fell at our feet, but we turned and ran
beyond the oyster shells and the stunted oak trees
to where the reeds were bending in the shallows
and a few crabs scuttled sideways through the sand
trailing paths of green fire that grew to tendrils,
tendrils to leaves, then phosphorescent branches
blossoming from our bodies as we swam
sideways against the current. When we stood
a moment on the farther shore, we saw
the lamplight beckoning us from the little windows,
and once again we waded into darkness
and swam, half afraid, through the strong, sea-going water
until we felt its slow release and rose
reborn on earth. Then when we walked the beach
our tracks still shone with a green instant fire,
and all that night we swam in a tide of stars,
and all that tide we bloomed in a tree of light.

44

## In the Pasture

It would be impossible to draw these three work horses
without a pencil of light
as they stand broadside to the afternoon sun
outlined with narrow lines of fire around their vast
chestnut forms, almost black against the dazzle.
The young mare swings her long tail from hip to hip,
and her Titian-blond mane hangs over her shoulder
like the ringletted chevelure of a Victorian belle,
innocent and alluring.
                              Beyond her
the two big geldings, brothers and team mates,
scratch each other's wide red backs
with careful incisors.
                              Swallows fly
over the grass, cloud shadows cross the lake
and darken the blue of the hills on the opposite shore
but in the pasture the sun is shining,
the afternoon wind has driven off the flies,
and the three big horses are all at their ease;
a small, happy society
of souls who are gentle and do no harm,
who live in God's pocket, who spend the long summer days
moving from sunshine to shade and back to the sun,
who want nothing but to be where they are.

## The Hay Rake

One evening I stopped by the field to watch the hay rake
drawn toward me by two black, tall, ponderous horses
who stepped like conquerors over the fallen oat stalks,
light-shot dust at their heels, long shadows before them.
At the ditch the driver turned back in a wide arc,
the off-horse scrambling, the near-horse pivoting neatly.
The big side-delivery rake came about with a shriek—
its tines were crashing, the iron-bound tongue groaned aloud—
then, Hup, Diamond! Hup, Duke! and they set off west,
trace-deep in dust, going straight into the low sun.

The clangor grew faint, distance and light consumed them;
a fiery chariot rolled away in a cloud of gold
and faded slowly, brightness dying into brightness.
The groaning iron, the prophesying wheels,
the mighty horses with their necks like storms—
all disappeared; nothing was left but a track
of dust that climbed like smoke up the evening wind.

## Talking to the Dog

When I used to get up in the morning
and make some funny noises—
jargon, bits of songs, nonsense—
I wasn't really talking to myself;
no, I was talking to the dog.

But now the dog is dead;
no more unkempt wolf-hound lying asleep on her back
with her legs against the wall.
I must say good-bye to her prehistoric howling,
good-bye to the look of those mad, yellow owl-eyes.
I drop her unfinished dinner onto the compost pile,
I wash her bowls and put them away,
I pull the rug over the place where her bed was;
and still I think I can hear her,
just stirring in the next room.

It is almost midsummer;
the blackberries are flowering in festoons beside the pasture;
I will bury her ashes under the crooked pear tree
with the fruit already growing among its green leaves.
I know that for a long time I will hear her at the door,
and see her out of the corner of my eye.
When the wind tracks light through the bending grass,
for a long time I will be talking to the dog.

## The Horses' Water

I turn on the horses' water from the tap by the
    back door
and away it flows, down across the grass, through
    two connected hoses
that thread through the little apple trees and creep
    under the pasture fence
to end with a head over the edge of the black
    rubber tub.
Down there it looks like a green snake drinking
    from a black well;
from up here it is a green seam stitching the
    lawn together.
In the evening I stand by the tap looking and
    looking
at the pale light that lingers in the west, at the
    shadowy garden,
the dark shapes of the horses, now barely to be seen,
(am I imagining them?) and the darker thicket
of alders below the pasture, where an owl hoots
    twice.

After a very long time the sky rises in the tub.

48

## Peaches

Jenny, because you are twenty-three
                    (and my daughter),
you think you know everything;
and because I am fifty-three
                    (and your mother),
I think *I* know everything.
A week ago you picked up two green little peaches,
only half-grown and still hard,
from under the loaded peach tree
and put them on the kitchen window sill;
and I thought
          (though I didn't say a word):
they're too small, they will just rot
but I won't move them, Jenny put them there.

Now the summer is over and you are gone,
the mornings are cool, squashes conquer the garden,
the tree swallows have flown away, crickets sing—
and the sweet juice of your peaches runs down my chin.

## Life Class

A white room upstairs,
two windows at the back, four panes to each sash,
and all of them distorted.
                              What can you see?
Sky, and a headland of green treetops, white houses,
slightly stretched and shimmering in the old glass—
there are masts rocking below them.
                              The model comes in
and pulls her light blue smock up over her head.
                                        Now draw
with faith: goldenrod and asters and Queen Anne's
lace, late red roses by the shore line, stones
and more stones, mackerel sky on top,
kelp at the tide's edge—
                              and someone
who still comes naked from the shining water.

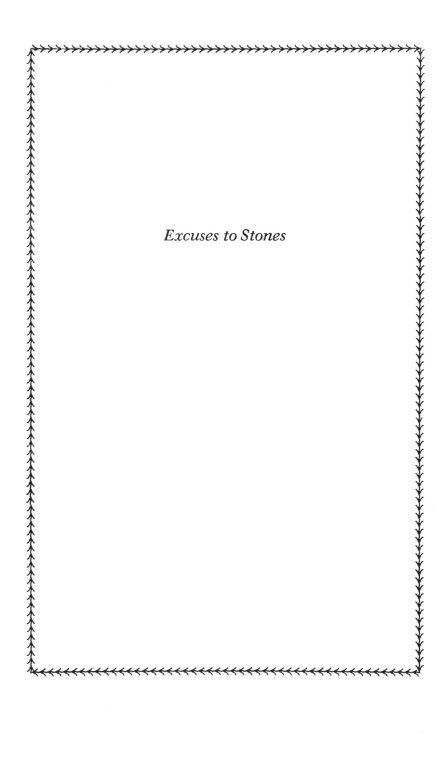

*Excuses to Stones*

## Where the Deer Were

It's always hard to form a true picture
of what is happening, isn't it?
Difficult to know what's what.

                       For instance,
the moving tenderness of the desiring man,
the gentle vanity of the desired woman
sliding their bare arms and legs together
in the grass across the stream.

                     It's late summer,
a misty day, but warm.

                I can't see their faces.
So what is happening, really?
Perhaps they are fighting—very evenly.
Perhaps those sounds are groans of pain.

                      Now the mist
closes my eyes.

           When it lifts once more,
I see nothing over there
but a hollow in the long grass
like the places where deer have been lying,
and the only thing I hear
is shallow water making excuses to stone.

## Shapes in the Cloud

The weathervane rider is beating and beating his horse
up under the clouds. My former husband
climbs into bed with his young wife thousands of miles
from here.
                I drive slowly away from land.
The Sheepscot River lies deep in drifting mist.
The two old hulks of schooners grounded on tidal
mud now float on top of the mist like real
ships again, like the swans they used to be
beyond living memory. The other side
of the channel is invisible, the bridge dips down
and ends in a thick question.
                      Shapes in the cloud—
dredgers working at the bottom of the river.

## Another Full Moon

The house, lit by moonlight
on the snow, glows inside
like a huge jewel, a moonstone
or opal.
       The whole house
shimmers with its freight
of living souls, and the souls
of disembodied memory.
               I lie
inside my warm bed in the cold
brightness, dreaming of those
who can no longer dream
of anyone, who have become
motes of dust
in the air, those universal
dreamers.
          You would imagine,
looking into the next room,
that a lamp was lit,
but I know it is only
the light of the moon
westering, nearly full,
over the snow.
             I am not wanting
or asking anything
impossible; it's just
that I can't help
thinking about it.

## The Blueberry Barrens

Asleep, I dreamed a door in the bedroom wall,
through it another room, more windows.
Don't look for the door, for the windows.
Outside those windows there is not another view;
looking through them, you will see the same
    fields of winter rye coming up,
the same flocks of cowbirds turning like a concerted thought:
nothing is waiting.

Looking back now from the opposite hill, I see my house
caught in the high branches of a leafless maple.
If I became a bird, if I flew up to that little gray house,
would there be a perch at the door for my bird feet?
Would the lamps still light, the piano make a tiny music?

Nothing is waiting;
it is all taking place right now.
I turn away from the house in the tree
and drive my black horse up the lane to the blueberry barrens
where the leaves run out of the sky like spilled claret
and a big hawk glides low over the bare ridge, almost touching.

## The Pasture Fence

Now the sky turns a bright, dark red as the sun drops near the horizon.
The colors of the hills deepen, the dry asters shine like stars
against the long drifts of wood shadow behind them. Some clouds
take the light, others stand blue before it; the bare tree tops
seem to be made from twisted gold wires.
                                          I go out
to carry hay to the black horse at the gate.
Walking into light, I see that the bright kingdom
has set its boundary just beyond our young apple trees.
The darkening lawn slopes down to it;
only the pasture fence divides that world from the world.

## Summer Night

There is a circle of dark red lilies
behind the two pear trees and dozens more
on the way up to the barn. As night comes on,
they become only darker presences in the gathering
darkness.
        The black horse
is loose; he wanders
among the thickly-flowering lily stalks
picking out the small starry heads
of white clover scattered in the lawn.
Venus hangs in the west like a drop of melting
gold, she looks yearningly across the sky
to red Mars slowly rising in the south.
And then the numberless stars come out, the night wind
breathes its warm sighs that smell of the old roses
still blooming in the long grass
above the ditch.
        As the sky darkens,
the bright half moon casts shadows. The old horse
lies down to sleep with his chin on the ground
by the well cover.
        All night, in the field below him,
whole galaxies of fireflies glitter and shift
like sparks of that fire that shines in everything,
like thoughts that are streaming through an infinite mind.

## Birds

The young swifts in the chimney chatter
and I hear the sigh of the parents' wings;
the chimney is like a breathing heart in the bedroom wall.

Rain is coming,
a loon calls his shaken cry from the lake.
I should like to send you

words like this rain that is just starting to fall—
soft rain of a summer evening—
words to say I have not forgotten

the ladder over the tin lean-to
up to that flat roof in the spring nights,
how it used to be

under the mad, round moon
that made the mockingbird sing until dawn,
how I hung backward over the parapet,

dizzy, swooping, trusting;
my heart was like wings in my throat,
my body was a bird's.

Now I stand at the farmhouse window
watching the swallows dip low over the grass tops.
It is years since I saw you,

and still the wings whisper in the wall
and the soft rain softly repeats:
Yes, it was so, yes, yes, it was so, it was so.

## The Other Room

Our neighbor, in his middle eighties, went up on the hill
to mow his blueberry fields. He covered the tractor
and started to walk down. In three days they found him
alive. He had had a bad time. When he knew he was
found again, tended, warm, wrapped up, looked after,
he slipped away quickly, he died.

                                   I suppose he felt
it was safe to die, he didn't have to fight it
any longer.
                I drove past his lonely house
on the dirt road. His two trucks, impossibly old,
waited like dogs. It was October, the stubble
stood green in his fields that ended in torn clouds
rising from the invisible river valley
below them and obscuring the lines of distant
and more distant hills. I could hear the stream
that runs through his dooryard. An apple tree,
still very heavy with fruit, leaned from the bank
like a cow with a full udder.
                           Where do our souls
go when they leave us? I thought I could feel his soul
right there.
               Last summer I waved to the old man
as he mowed the long grass by the stream, askew
on his tractor seat, leaning far sideways, and yet
getting well into the corners. He waved back proudly
as if to say, "You see how I'm managing here,
how I keep going." Now all the neighbors call it
a hard death, as earlier they had called
his life a hard one. He had such a reputation
for courage and stubbornness that I wonder if he
might not have preferred it this way to leaving
for any hospital.

I drove by his place a few weeks
later. The leaves were off the trees. The battered
trucks hadn't moved. Everything seemed exactly
the same, but I felt as though he weren't there
any longer. I remembered the poet Blake
saying he could not think of death as more
than the going out of one room into another.
And hadn't our old neighbor gone on into
the other room at last?
                            **What other room?**
When I came home that night, the three-quarter moon
was shining straight into the dead man's pond
beyond its thicket of beeches. The cold, still water
shone up from the dark ground as if it were all
light, as if its blue fire were all there is.

## The Stairs

Midway on the overgrown wood road,
a farmhouse used to stand.
It has fallen down.
Nothing is left there but the stairs
going up in the air by themselves.
Today, at the end of September,
the yellow maple leaves drift sideways
and gather on the sagging steps
once worn by so many footfalls
but now abandoned like ancient tribesmen
left behind on the bank of a river
they could no longer cross.
                   A Micmac sorcerer
said the gods lived in the air,
a little higher than the trees. Perhaps
that's still true. Perhaps it was here
that a man lay with his head on a stone
watching the angels
climbing the stairs as clouds do
on a rising wind, as the winter stars
pause one moment on the black edge
of the sky—and then step upward.

## Dove Sono

I thought it was the prettiest day of the year
or maybe ever, like sitting up in bed
with your lover, saying that was the best time, the trees
leafed out in their different greens, the wild cherries blooming
in a way to convince anyone that the wood
was half made of cherry trees.
                                    The islands
lay blue in a veiled air
where a warm wind was turning up small waves,
white on the wrinkling water,
as I drove up the coast hearing the car radio
sing about Figaro's marriage. *Dove sono?*
asked the sad countess. Nothing is lost,
my heart answered, everything
is necessary—but I knew
that what we were really doing was just
talking about our luck.
                            At the top of the hill,
the road fell away before me, turning
into a village street. The square white houses
stood there among apple blossoms
by a harbor as blue as a hyacinth petal
in the afternoon light, the headlands stretching
darker beyond it.
                        In my rear view mirror,
a car suddenly appeared, veering wildly
from side to side, then hurtling out of control
off the bank, all in seconds. I went back
and found it lying overturned
on a lawn below, a woman in the door of the house
saying the ambulance was coming, two men running
out of the woods with set faces.
Inside the upside down old car
no one was moving, nobody
was making a sound. One bent arm
stuck out from the driver's window looking white
on its vulnerable turned up underside, a man's
young arm that never stirred.

Oh, it is like that
on a spring day when that great space-traveller,
the sun, has carried us around the year
once more and there is such an effervescence
of fresh life all about us and in ourselves
that we rise on the songs of the mating birds, the scent
of the flowering trees; and sometimes this elixir
goes so strongly to our heads that we are ready
to toss it from the glass—as if we were
so in love with suddenness
that we could die for it like young
Phaethon, the boy whose name means "shining,"
standing alone in the chariot of his father,
the sun, careening through the grieved sky
shouting, and whipping on the burning horses.

# The Leaves

In the San Gabriel hills, it's always summer
because the leaves are never off the trees.
Lovers there lie twined under the live-oaks,
music plays in the winter stream beds.
New leaves on the sycamores, like small, green hands,
each hold a patch of cliff or a minute piece
of the sky.
        I went there once. The mountains
hovered on the horizon at evening, and later
the full moon shone in the mist
at my horse's shoulder so that he seemed to plunge
through a rocking surf of light. I lay in the arms
of a leaf-green man and floated in the trough
behind the waves.

        Are you ready?
What happens then?

        The long, gold light
of a low sun shining through glassy leaves
in another time—oh, hundreds
of years ago—where two mounted figures
gallop away down a shadowy alley of branches
in a *tapisserie verdure*.
        The branches caught
at my hands, the leaves
blinded me. When you are flying,
you should always hold on tight to the angel
whose wings are carrying you;
and still, you know, you could fall;
you might suddenly find yourself on the ground
with blood in your mouth, and your eyes snapped open wide.

## The Logging Sled

I catch a ride on the logging sled and go out to the woods.
As we cross the deep-drifted field, we see five snow geese
high overhead, flying almost confusedly.
It's early yet, the lake is still frozen tight
with trucks on it; the geese must be casting about
for open rivers north of us.

                  In the clearing
I step up to the horses' heads and stand with them
while the sled is loaded. I am as gray and heavy
as a badger, the pockets of my old coat sag
with carrots and books. The horses nose at my hands,
the wood thunks onto the sled, and I hear the blue jays
squalling behind me among the pines; I smell
a dampness in the air that promises spring.

To whom can I say how happy this all makes me?

*Time Out*

# The Barn in December

A few flakes of snow are blowing like stars, the stars
glisten like ice. The cold wind cuts and sings.
Above my head the weathervane creaks in the frozen
light of the waxing moon.
                              I push the barn door
open and go in. The stalls are full of whickering
dragons breathing out smoke and calling for feed.
I fill the pails at the pump, I carry the grain
from the zinc-lined cooler, then I climb to the mow.
Heavy and soft, six bales of hay fly down
like descending angels. The hollow nave is filled
with the smell of timothy, the sound of animals chewing.
I stand there for a moment enjoying their
pleasure, the sheltering peace of the wooden cave.

How many shingles has this barn been through?
How many floors? For almost two hundred years
its square timbers and its thin patched walls
have been standing up to the wind, have been holding off
the bitter cold, the great night of the whirling
darkness.
                  Now, once again, it is that time
of year when the cold triumphs, the night rules.
Every day the sun rises farther away.
It is hard to imagine him halting his march to the south,
stopping a little, resting in the black whirlwind
of space to take new form, to be born again,
in a barn.
                  But the shadowy barn has seen it happen
over and over, almost two hundred times.
The cast is still correct, the kindly horses
kneel as they fold down into their straw, the hens
roost in the rafters. Standing in the middle
of the threshing floor, I feel the rightness of it:
the calm of those generations of beasts, the power of other
hands on the beams, the light of the magic child
shining once more from the gathered summer of the hay.

## Time Out

In January
the year, which has been breathing in since midsummer,
holds its breath for a moment
before it begins to exhale.
And nothing happens!
The snow falls;
the snow plow doesn't get here;
the horses stay in the barn telling stories to one
    another;
the days pass, and no one gets any older.
Today it is zero outside, with a groaning northeast wind;
the snow is flying so thickly that the windows are quite
    dark.
My house feels like a warm hollow in a drift,
and I give myself up to its pleasures—
keeping lots of wood in the stove, boiling beans all day,
playing the piano, reading *Gilgamesh* once again,
and feeling completely safe
because the world cannot harm anyone while I stay here,
dark inside the whiteness,
and light inside the darkness,
neither coming nor going,
neither working nor playing,
neither awake nor asleep.

## January Morning

At eight in the morning it was five below;
there was ice glazed over the snow.
The distant fields looked like insets of mother-of-pearl
and the whole landscape was tinted like Boucher's wanton girl
sprawled belly-down on a sofa, the sky as delicately blue
as the shadows under her buttocks, a rosy hue
lingering at the horizon, the rest all white—
a silky candy-box painting that still carried a slight
luxurious smell of good chocolate:
                                        but soon the cold
made me stop thinking about that and I took hold
of the frozen reins to drive off in the pung.
The bells on the thills sounded where they hung,
four on each chime, small, and then large, and then small,
happy to be there ringing, happy to be there at all.

## Bear Trees

In February,
all of a sudden, there's a lot more light,
and it's a warm light.
                              Snow melts off the roof,
the hens start laying, the mare comes into season.
The early lambs are born in the barn cellar
where they bleat to their mothers in the half darkness
like the bulbs that are stirring in the full dark
underground. On the southern windowsill,
the old geraniums push out new stalks
and hang them with brick-pink blossoms.
Every day I find I wake up earlier,
my bones cracking as I sit up to stretch.
                                    Now the sap
is running, and this morning,
when I drove the pung up to the woodlot,
I saw three young maple trees
deeply scored with new bear scratches.

Oh warm light,
couldn't you have waited a little longer?
How safe we were in the dead of winter!
How softly we dreamed!
How beautiful it was to sleep under the snow!

## The Flowering Branch

In the February sliver of our lives,
we rode with one hand on the reins, the other
holding the earliest twig of five-petaled blossoms
pulled from the opening peach, a twisted
scar of green sap like lightning its memento.
We left the tree and, with the stolen scepter,
rode through the rivers of that stony land,
scattering circles of silver from our stirrups
while our horses' hoofs struck sparks.
                           And we had only
to shake the fragile blossoms in the air,
to hurry time and know before their birth
the impetuous greenness and the scarlet flowers
that sprang out of the stones. Then, once again,
the skeletons that lay about the path
were filled with coursing blood, and the taut skin
covered the whitened bones. A dog rose howling,
a foolish sheep scrambled up to its knees
and dashed away, while hares pocked deep with maggots
screamed with the resurrection and the life.
We had turned giddy with the rocketing
of our brown horses on the whirling ground;
we shook the branch in circles over our heads
until the petals flew in rings of smoke
above the fire of our lives, the edge of invisible
flame that rose from our breath—and it was then
the stolen flowers fell, and we were left
alone on panting horses in a land
of rocks and bones with nothing but a rod.

## Climbing March Hill

The river brawls under the bridge with its
water, that runs as black-green as an old
shutter, creased into white rapids. The banks
    still show as two thin
    white lines of icy

snow on the edges. Looking down from the
steep road up the hill, I see the black roofs
of the houses, lines of tarmac, the dark
    mass of the pine trees
    below the graveyard,

and the afternoon light—so much more of
that now!—seeming to stay, seeming as though
it could not move at all as it lodges
    in the bare topmost
    twigs of these maples

that are rose-colored with the late sun and
the flush of the living sap traveling
through their veins, tapped all around the massive
    trunks by tin buckets
    with folded covers

so that the patient trees look like emblems
of generosity, many-breasted
Ephesian Dianas with their rough bark
    dripping watery
    sweetness and their flanks

melting the old snow. A slow drift of smoke
trails over the slopes across the river
where someone is burning land; crows fly back
    and forth, getting their
    horrible tidbits

out of the ashes. But already we
must turn away from the toy-like village—
which has fallen a long way below us
        and now stands dimly
        in the deep shadow—

to go up the last steep slopes, while three small
blue mountain-tops rise behind us, and on
into the woods where a narrow stream runs
        among cedars, and
        a black bear sometimes

crosses, where the road first becomes a dark
branchy tunnel and then comes out onto
the high, bare ridge top where the unchecked wind
        blows the clouds all day
        long across the sky.

## The Buggies

"When I first began to practice,"
said the veterinarian, giving
a shot to the new foal, "this countryside
was full of old carriages. The barns
all had some, you could buy
a good top buggy for ten dollars. But now
a lot of the barns have fallen down
onto them. Those old farmers
used to hang their good buggies from the rafters,
safe and out of the way. And some people
went on using them a long time.
                                    I remember
one place in Warren," he said, putting iodine
on the umbilicus, watched anxiously
by the mare with her flickering eyes, "they had
this perfect drop-front phaeton. The top
was always up, the seat was plum-colored wool
with a cloth cover over it. Beautiful.
The old lady wouldn't go to church
in anything else.
                        But now that I think of it,
she must be gone too; the last time I was by there
the barn roof was down.
                                    They were
nice, those old things—
well made, you know.
They could stand up to a lot."
                                    He climbed
into his white truck and drove away,
ratttling down the lane. Behind, in the barn,
the mare nickered once as her foal began to nurse
and was silent.

The cold March evening
was darkening toward night, the patterns
of old snow made stripes in the dusk, the stars
were slowly coming out, but the lake
at the bottom of the hill went on picking up
the last daylight. Its surface glowed
softly as if it were lighted
from below, as if a distant sun were submerged there
under the ice, still shining, alive, and warm.

## Spring Again: California

Spring again. The old dog goes out courting
and comes home at last torn, hungry, and lame.
Buck-brush flowers like smoke across the hills
guarded by the stinging sparks of wild bees
while the orange orchards in the valley bloom
and bear at once, drugging the light air
with a stuporous sweetness.
                                        Now dusty hens
lay their white eggs once more, and the testy cocks
pick quarrels, thrusting out their neck feathers
in a fiery circle around small, fierce heads.
Their brazen voices rise in continual challenge;
the underbrush shakes with their constant battles
and its pale new leaves are stained with the dark blood
of maddened heroes driven by their fates
as the green plains that once surrounded Troy
Even the peaceful geldings in the pasture,
sleek once again in a week with the new grass,
rear suddenly to spar at one another
with their armored hoofs, half playful and half not.

I, too, the imperfect animal, can't help feeling it,
within and without, the unrest and the amorous surge,
and wonder: did lovely Beauty rise from the deep
tide into tossed spray and blowing roses
to set the dewy world at odds with itself
and send gentle Persephone home to us
trailing her garlands on the arm of Strife?

## April and then May

April and then May,
violets up in the field,
the ewes with their twin lambs;

time has decided
to turn into spring again
after all.

The maples are unfolding their leaves,
chives stand green at the kitchen door,
the black flies have decided to come back;

and the work mare has her new foal
capering over bluets in the pasture,
and the hall smells of daffodils;

and everything
is divinely ordinary—
the deep ruts in the field track,

the spring overflowing,
the excited swallows,
the apple trees

budding for perhaps the hundredth time—
and the pruned boughs budding too
that must bloom just where they lie.

## Well Water

While the horses strain at the harrow in a darkening field,
   I pour red wine over lentils in an iron kettle.
The full moon rising beyond the farm graveyard is as round as a well,
   and the cold autumn wind has the taste of distant water.

## About the Author

The daughter of Henry Beston and Elizabeth Coatsworth, Kate Barnes
spent her childhood years in Maine and Massachusetts. She now
lives on a farm in coastal Maine, in the same area her father
made famous in *Northern Farm*. Her poetry has appeared
in numerous publications, including *Harpers*,
*The New Yorker*, *The Village Voice*,
*The New England Review*,
and *Harvard Review*.

## About the Illustrator

Mary Azarian, a graduate of Smith College, grew up in Virginia and
presently lives in Vermont. Her woodcut prints have appeared in
*A Farmer's Alphabet*, *Sea Gifts*, and *The Tale of
John Barleycorn*, and her illustrations in
*The Man Who Lived Alone*,
all published by Godine.

*Where the Deer Were*

was set on the Linotype by The Ascensius Press of South Portland, Maine, in Intertype Waverly. Drawn by George Trenholm, Waverly is based on the designs of Justus Erich Walbaum, a typefounder active in Germany in the early nineteenth century. Waverly is close in spirit to the refined and attenuated types first introduced by Firmin Didot, designs that accentuated the thicks and thins, carried the stress along a horizontal rather than a diagonal axis, and were cut along fairly strict geo-metrical principles. Waverly is more subtle than these French faces, its contours softened by the sensitivity of the handcraftsman who cut it, and its sharp angularities modified by the influence of Pierre Simon Fournier's transitional designs.

*The book has been printed by Capital City Press, Montpelier, Vermont, on Glatfelter Offset Eggshell, an entirely acid-free paper.*